# ZEN
INSPIRATIONS

# ZEN INSPIRATIONS

MIRIAM LEVERING

ESSENTIAL MEDITATIONS AND TEXTS

WATKINS PUBLISHING
LONDON

**Zen Inspirations**
Text selection and introduction by Miriam Levering
Foreword by Lucien Stryk

First published in the United Kingdom and Ireland in 2000 by
Duncan Baird Publishers Ltd
Sixth Floor, Castle House
75–76 Wells Street
London W1T 3QH

This paperback edition first published in 2011 by Watkins Publishing,
an imprint of Duncan Baird Publishers Ltd

Conceived, created and designed by Duncan Baird Publishers



Editor: Joanne Levêque
Designer: Dan Sturges
Picture researchers: Emily Stone and Cecilia Weston-Baker
Commissioned calligraphy: Yukki Yaura

British Library Cataloguing-in-Publication Data:
A catalogue record for this book is available from the British Library

Library of Congress Cataloging-in-Publication Data

Levering, Miriam, 1945-
Zen inspirations : essential meditations and texts / Miriam Levering. -- First paperback edition.
pages cm
"Text selection and introduction by Miriam Levering. Foreword by Lucien Stryk."
"First published in the United Kingdom and Ireland in 2000 by Duncan Baird
Publishers Ltd."
ISBN 978-1-907486-94-4
1. Zen meditations. I. Title.
BQ9289.5.L48 2011
294.3'4432--dc22

2010043332

1 3 5 7 9 10 8 6 4 2

Typeset in Nofret and Stone Sans
Colour reproduction by Colourscan, Singapore
Printed in Malaysia for Imago

Note on abbreviations:
The abbreviations CE and BCE are used throughout this book:
CE Common Era (the equivalent of AD)
BCE Before the Common Era (the equivalent of BC)

Distributed in the USA and Canada by
Sterling Publishing Co., Inc.
387 Park Avenue South
New York, NY 10016-8810

For information about custom editions, special sales, premium and corporate
purchases, please contact Sterling Special Sales Department at 800-805-5489
or specialsales@sterlingpub.com.

# CONTENTS

# PREFACE

This book is an illustrated selection of major Zen writings–an alliance of photographic and verbal eloquence that aims to capture something of the spirit of Zen, providing a unique stimulus for meditation and contemplation.

Dr. Miriam Levering has selected two major landmarks of Zen literature–*The Gateless Gate* koan collection and the *Ox-herding Pictures* with their verses (alongside the original paintings, reproduced in color). In addition she has chosen some of the finest Zen poetry. Her selection includes translations of classic Zen texts by Lucien Stryk, the esteemed poet and Zen practitioner, who has contributed an illuminating and reflective foreword to the book. Dr. Levering's own historical introduction to Zen literature, philosophy, and concepts (pages 11 to 19) offers fascinating insights into the origins and traditions that lie behind the simplicity, directness, wisdom, and humor that is Zen.

The photographs included in the book are intended to resonate with, rather than directly illustrate, the texts. Readers are invited to open their imaginations to the alliance of text and image, and let the wisdom of each gradually permeate the mind. Many of the texts–especially the koans–are enigmatic and paradoxical. The most fruitful approach is not to seek to overintellectualize, as if solving a crossword puzzle, but instead to let the insight sink into consciousness, in the belief that a resolution will, in its own time, surface. For this reason, and because no one can pretend to offer tidy interpretations of Zen, the texts are presented without any modern commentary. However, some helpful literary background is given on pages 12 to 15 and a glossary of terms on pages 156 to 157.

# FOREWORD

LUCIEN STRYK

Mostly, we lollop around the universe, scarcely knowing who we are. Moments, hours, years, centuries, we slither between savagery and love, calamity and calm, indifference and pity, unsure of the Way, trapped in our own making of ourselves. Fraught with anxiety, frustration, not liking what we see, we wonder how to find contentment and peace in such a complex world. There are some who dedicate a lifetime to the search for answers, seek through the litter of the ages, turn from the mess we make and remake of things, and that is what this book is all about–a graceful introduction to awareness, with illuminating images, essential words.

My friend, the late Zen poet Shinkichi Takahashi (whose poem *Shell* appears on page 66), would have been happy to know he was part of this book–a thoughtfully unified collection, giving page by page a true insight into the spirit and philosophy by which he lived.

From time to time, sipping tea beneath his *inka* (a Zen master's testimonial that his disciple had won through to awakening) I would draw from Takahashi, albeit reluctantly, the koans that his Zen master, Shizan Ashikaga, had set for him in the time-honored tradition of Zen training (page 17) and that had inspired his poetry. One of these koans was "Describe your face before you were begotten by your parents." Takahashi's response was this *agyo* (poem of mutual understanding), *Collapse:*

> Time oozed from my pores,
> Drinking tea
> I tasted the seven seas.

I saw in the mist formed
Around me
The fatal chrysanthemum, myself.

Its scent choked, and as I
Rose, squaring
My shoulders, the earth collapsed.

After a period of intense meditation, and many failures, suddenly those words came. He saw that face as if for the first time, was overwhelmed, realized he had looked for a lifetime without understanding, and felt liberated.

Zen poems, whether written now or in the far past, are notable for the insight they offer. The eighth-century Chinese master Beirei, for example, all those centuries ago, asserted that the only thing worth looking deeply into is oneself in the here and now, that a mind bogged in a system is, inevitably, led to inflexible presuppositions, whereas meditation and pure perception can lead into the very nature of things. He would have found truth in the saying of the Chinese master, Ch'ing-yuan (660–740):

Before I had studied Zen I saw mountains as mountains,
waters as waters. When I learned something of Zen,
the mountains were no longer mountains, waters no longer waters.
But now that I understand Zen, I am at peace with myself,
seeing mountains once again as mountains, waters as waters.

The texts and photographs in this book are very much, in spirit and texture, like *shigajiku* (combined poems and paintings). A good example appears on pages 48 to 49–the poems by Lady Chiyo-Jo and Kikaku:

In the well bucket
a morning glory–
I borrow water.

Leaf
of the yam–
raindrop's world.

In less sensitive hands the poems might have turned up alongside an obvious well and bucket, or, as bad, a pile of yams. Instead we have droplets of water on, maybe, a fallen leaf. Another fine example can be found on page 51, where the photograph accompanies to breathtaking effect Buson's

> A sudden chill–
> in our room my dead wife's
> comb, underfoot.

Together how well they illustrate Zen's "less is more." The poem is bare. In order to appreciate it we must feel for the dead wife, and for the poet. We are struck by the absence of detail; this is a very personal, spontaneous experience, but paradoxically richer for being so. We must create for ourselves that special room, a certain comb, hear the sound as it is trodden upon–and turning to the photograph see the empty floorboards.

The editors of Zen have fine-tuned each page to a marvel of unity. The poems resonate, leading through *The Gateless Gate* to the *Ox-herding Pictures*. Altogether this is indeed a fruitful approach to a discipline whose words and images are as alive today as fifteen hundred years ago. The thirteenth-century master Dogen wrote:

> This slowly drifting cloud is pitiful:
> What dreamwalkers men become.
> Awakened, I hear the one true thing–
> Black rain on the roof of Fukakusa Temple.

We can see an image of ourselves in raindrops, catch a laugh line on the belly of a hill, stare into hungry eyes in doorways, watch a falling leaf add to the tapestry of pavements. Or open this book at random. There is compassion, revelation, light, pure thought in everything, in Zen.

Lucien Stryk

# INTRODUCTION

## DR. MIRIAM LEVERING

Of the many types of Buddhism that are practiced in Asia today, Zen is one of the most familiar to a Western audience. Perhaps we are attracted to Zen's practical approach to spirituality and the value it places on personal experience and intuition, perhaps to Zen's directness and humor, or perhaps to the simplicity and elegance of its arts. Or maybe the appeal of Zen is simply what Zen adherent Alan Watts (1915–1973) described as Zen's "sense of beauty and nonsense, at once exasperating and delightful."

This book is intended as an introduction to the enigma and subtle harmony of Zen and as a contemplative aid for the lay reader. Like all Zen literature, the writings collected in this anthology are concerned with the search for and the attainment of enlightenment–the realization of one's true nature. *The Gateless Gate* koan collection and the poems that accompany the *Ox-herding Pictures* are classic tools (still used today in Zen monastic training) that form a good starting-point for readers interested in exploring this ancient tradition. Drawing upon the great wealth of Zen poetry that exists–from the poems of early Chinese masters to the short Japanese poems known as haiku and the work of modern poets–the selection presented here offers glimpses of the serenity and freedom of accomplished Zen practitioners.

The vast wealth of Zen literature falls into two broad categories. The first of these comprises historical records of the sayings and doings of Zen masters as well as the koan literature derived from these records (page 13). The second category comprises a wide range of poetry covering both poems composed by awakened Zen masters and poems recognized by them as expressing Zen (page 12).

## THE POEMS (PAGES 20 TO 69)

Verse has long been vitally important in Zen, as truths that cannot be expressed in doctrine or prose can be hinted at in poetry. Much Zen poetry is produced in religious and ritual contexts; beyond this, it is any poetry that is recognized by Zen masters as conveying real wisdom and compassion.

Early Zen poems served a variety of purposes. Some were expressions of the central insight attained at the moment of enlightenment, or awakening; others were composed by a Zen master to be inscribed on a portrait of himself or were written in honor of a famous predecessor. In the seventeenth century the Japanese Zen monk Matsuo Basho (1644–1694) gave Zen a distinctive poetic form, later called haiku. These brief seventeen-syllable poems are intended to produce sudden insights that free the reader from seeing the world in a conventional way. Many such poems simultaneously describe the beauty of the natural world and suggest the poet's own experience of enlightenment.

Other common themes in Zen poetry include the coexistence of apparent opposites, such as being and nonbeing, stillness and motion, and life and death. The themes of poverty and aloneness also feature strongly, symbolizing, in an apparent paradox, the poet's awareness of his or her spritual wealth and oneness with the universe. Recurring metaphors include the vast and empty sky as an image of the uncluttered nature of the awakened mind, and the moon, representing one's enlightened true nature.

The selection presented here spans thirteen centuries of Zen poetic writing and includes examples of several forms: enlightenment poems, death poems (the deathbed sayings of Zen masters, page 33), haiku (pages 46 to 54), and modern pieces. All are written by Zen masters and students (see the chronological list of major Zen figures on page 158).

### *THE GATELESS GATE* (PAGES 70 TO 143)

The first recording of "public cases" (*kung-an*, koan) was undertaken, so far as we know, in the ninth century. After this, for teaching purposes, a number of masters compiled collections of the koans most useful for study. *The Gateless Gate* (also called *Wu-men-kuan*, or *Mumonkan*) was written by Wu-men Hui-k'ai (1183–1260), also known as Mumon Ekai, or simply Mumon, a Zen monk and master of the Rinzai school (page 19). *The Gateless Gate* is regarded as the most accessible of the major Chinese collections. Most contemporary Japanese masters prefer students to begin with this collection, which consists of forty-eight koans, each accompanied by a brief commentary and poem added by Mumon to provide guidance for the student.

A koan is a "riddle" with no apparent answer. It is used to train the mind to attain enlightenment (*kensho* or *satori*) in a sudden flash by guiding a person to think about the world in new ways. Koans, which are unique to Zen Buddhism, usually take the form of apparently absurd statements made during conversations between a teacher and student. Koans are not nonsense; the realization toward which they point makes a deep kind of sense. Koans are concerned with the ways in which such apparent opposites as self and other, the eternal and the temporary, the universal and the particular, are united in every moment of our experience.

Koans are used to test Buddhist perception and insight and to evaluate teachers and students alike. Students are traditionally assigned a koan to work on and then move on to the next one when the teacher considers that they have "solved" it.

### THE *OX-HERDING PICTURES* (pages 144 TO 155)

The *Ox-herding Pictures*, which complete this anthology, are accompanied by ten poems composed by the Chinese monk K'uo-an Shih-yuan in the twelfth

century. The ox represents the mind that must be tamed and trained. The ten pictures and poems symbolize the stages an individual passes through on the path to enlightenment. Over the centuries other sets of images and accompanying verses have appeared portraying the mind as the ox and the student of Zen as the herder, but this version is the most popular one in Japanese Zen. The ox-herding images reproduced in this volume were painted by the fifteenth-century Japanese Zen monk Shubun.

## THE AWAKENED MIND

Buddhists of the Great Vehicle or Mahayana, to which Zen belongs, believe that one's own experience shows that all objects of perception and thought are not permanent but come into being when other necessary conditions for their existence are fulfilled. In this sense, all objects of thought and perception have no independent existence. And if things have no definite boundaries that make them independently and permanently themselves, then we must see them as being caused, not just by a few other things at any given time, but ultimately by all other things at once.

Buddhists call things that have no permanent substance or definite boundaries "empty" things. The central paradox of everything we experience in life is that it is truly empty and at the same time possessed of a marvelous, subtle, mysterious existence. Everything is empty, yet spring comes, flowers bloom, and trees show new growth. Everything is empty, yet even the most ordinary thing is marvelous in itself. Zen masters teach that to realize the emptiness and interconnectedness of all things, not just with the mind but with one's whole being, is to achieve enlightenment–to become a Buddha.

Throughout its history Zen has focused on the search for enlightenment through oral teachings, meditation practice, and sustained personal reflection on the meaning of sayings and dialogues. The search for awakening can be traced back to early Indian Buddhism, in which attaining *dhyana*, or inner stillness, was understood to be a crucial step on the path to enlightenment. The discipline of cultivating this profoundly peaceful mind was undertaken along with a second discipline called "cultivating wisdom." This involved learning to see clearly exactly what one perceives, feels, and thinks just as it is, without placing an extra layer of emotional coloring or intellectual interpretation on top of experience, as we normally do. An individual who has a good foundation in both of these disciplines is ready to leap to enlightenment.

## DISCOVERING THE GIFTS WE ALREADY HAVE

In Zen, enlightenment, or profound inner peace, is not understood as something that we have to work hard to attain. Rather, it is seen as the true character of the awakened mind that is already fully present in each of us. Wisdom and peace of mind are not mutually contradictory, nor are they achievements, but given in everyone. The challenge, then, is to discover the gifts that we already have. Awakened awareness is like being in love, when there seems to be no possible barrier between oneself and the other–in this case, all others. And yet one's sense of self is not obliterated but transformed and heightened. The awakened mind is often compared to an empty mirror that reflects everything perfectly and responds to everything appropriately. An awakened person has an inner peace and stillness on the one hand, and a joyful, energetic liveliness on the other.

According to Zen belief, deluded mind–the opposite of awakened mind–is a very powerful force. It separates us from the world and from others and convinces us that we have to defend the "self." It produces reactions in the body, the mind, and the emotions to whatever comes up, reactions that we identify with "myself." To make headway against deluded mind, one needs to experience moments in which one is present to oneself without the activity of deluded mind. To make large strides against it, one needs to have real insight into its emptiness and unreality. When deluded mind is broken through, practitioners experience a powerful flash of insight into the essential nature of all existence, the oneness that is beyond all description. In Japanese Rinzai traditions such a moment is called *kensho* or *satori*. Moments of *satori* are described in many of *The Gateless Gate* koans.

## THE ZEN TEACHING METHOD

The Zen teaching method centers on the dialogue between master and student. In China, the words and actions of one's own Zen master became more important than Buddhist scriptures as a way to encounter the mind of a Buddha at work. Traditionally, students would travel from master to master in the hope that an encounter would trigger awakening. In Zen stories, the master assumes the role of a judge in a courtroom where the student is up for trial. If the student fails to display Zen understanding and an awakened mind, he is sent away or given thirty blows.

According to the beliefs of the Rinzai Zen school, the student can make progress only through intense doubt highly focused on a single knotty problem. This problem can be one that emerges directly from the student's life or one that arises from his or her struggle to understand the words and actions of a master as recorded in a koan, or "public case." The first koan in *The Gateless Gate* provides the student with a doubt-focusing single word, *mu* (nothingness, closely related to emptiness). Understanding what is meant by *mu* is often used as the first challenge in the Rinzai koan curriculum today.

## THE ORIGINS OF ZEN

Zen has its roots in Indian Buddhism and began in China but it remains best known as a distinctively Japanese form of Buddhism. The name Zen comes from the word *Ch'an*–a shortened form of the Chinese transliteration of the Indian word *dhyana*, which means a profound inner stability and stillness of mind reached in meditation.

According to Zen's account of its own history, its teachers are descended in a direct line from the Buddha and his disciple Mahakasyapa in India. This line continued through twenty-eight generations to Bodhidharma, an Indian monk who brought Zen to China in *c.*520 CE. Bodhidharma found a worthy successor in a Chinese monk named Hui-k'o, and the Zen lineage has continued to the present day, spreading from China to Korea, Vietnam, Japan, and now around the world. The story of Bodhidharma's transmission of enlightenment to Hui-k'o is a classic Zen tale (page 130). Hui-k'o, who had studied other Buddhist teachings, stood at the door to Bodhidharma's cave all night in the snow, hoping that Bodhidharma would grant him an interview. When Bodhidharma finally asked him what he wanted, Hui-k'o said, "My mind is not at peace." Bodhidharma said, "Find your mind and bring it to me, and I will make it peaceful for you." After a long pause, Hui-k'o answered, "I can't find my mind." Bodhidharma replied, "There, I have pacified it for you."

Three hundred years after Hui-k'o, ninth-century Zen teachers in China created the teaching style that is reflected in *The Gateless Gate*. Teachers began to use cryptic statements, shouts, and beatings to jolt their students out of ordinary habits of thinking and into a new awakened awareness. During the tenth century, Zen masters assigned accounts of the dialogues between earlier teachers and students ("public cases", or koans) as meditation subjects. By the twelfth century this teaching technique had developed still further: masters encouraged novices studying the koans to focus their minds on a single puzzling story, phrase, or even word until awakening occurred.

It was during the Sung period (960–1276), when Zen became the dominant Buddhist practice in China, that Japanese monks traveled to China to study before returning to Japan to establish Zen schools. These monks included Eisai (also called Yosai, 1141–1215), who visited China and brought back Rinzai Zen, and Dogen (1200–1253), who founded the Soto Zen school, which soon became one of the largest Buddhist sects in Japan. Rinzai Zen became known for its use of the koan as a tool leading to sudden enlightenment, while Soto Zen emphasized the importance of *zazen* (seated meditation), through which enlightenment could be realized gradually.

## ZEN IN THE MODERN WORLD

The individualism of our modern culture and the lessening of the influence of conventional religions have created the conditions in which new religious and spiritual paths appeal to those searching for meaning. Since the early twentieth century, Zen has attracted many Westerners. Robert Aitken, Philip Kapleau, D. T. Suzuki, and Alan Watts are among the pioneers who have presented Zen in ways that we can appreciate and make our own.

Centers of Zen study and practice have grown up around the world, offering a quiet, disciplined approach to self-knowledge and a steadily growing freedom from the entanglements produced by greed and fear. Zen teaches not a way to escape oneself or the world, but a way to look deeply and carefully at every moment of one's experience. Such persistent questioning appeals to many of us.

The aesthetic of Zen has also proved to hold great appeal. Zen paintings, calligraphy, gardens, flower arrangements, the tea ceremony, and architecture articulate the relation between the universal and the particular, form and emptiness, and mind, body, and nature. As in much Zen poetry, a sense of the mysterious, overwhelming beauty of nature pervades all Zen teaching and this is undoubtedly attractive to those of us who are eager to rediscover the close links between ourselves and the natural world.

# 偈頌

POEMS

**I make my home in the mountains**

You ask why I live
alone in the mountain forest,

and I smile and am silent
until even my soul grows quiet:

it lives in the other world,
one that no one owns.

The peach trees blossom.
The water continues to flow.

**Li Po**
(701–762)

Seclude the mind, not the movements,
remain living in the world of man.
Lack a tree? Plant a sapling.
Without a mountain? Look at a picture.
Living amidst clamor I am not flustered;
true meaning is found in this.

**Ch'iao-jan**
(734–*c.*792)

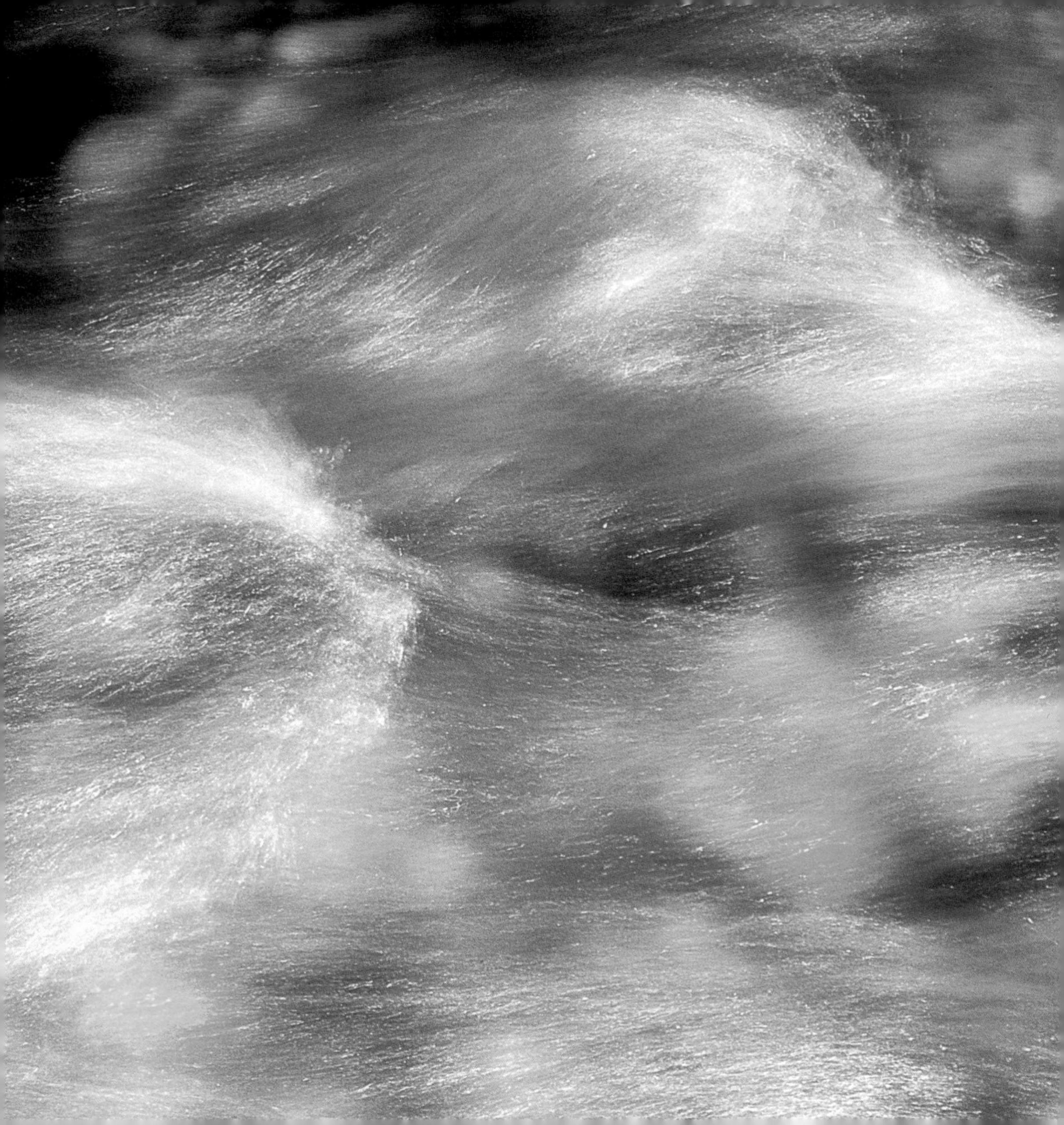

## Lute

My lute set aside
  on the little table,
lazily I meditate
  on cherished feelings.
The reason I don't bother
  to strum and pluck?
There's a breeze over the strings
  and it plays itself.

**Po Chu-i**
(772–846)

Green mountains father white clouds:
white clouds are the children of mountains.
White clouds hang around all day.
Mostly the mountain doesn't mind.

**T'ung-shan Liang-chieh**
(807–869)

Clouds appear free of care
and carefree drift away.
But the carefree mind is not to be "found"—
to find it, first stop looking around.

**Wang An-shih**
(1021–1086)

Earth, river, mountain:
snowflakes melt in air.
How could I have doubted?
Where's north? south? east? west?

**Dangai**
(*c.*1127–1279)

Sixty-six years
piling sins,
I leap into hell—
above life and death.

**T'ien-t'ung Ju-ching**
(1183–1228)

Four and fifty years
I've hung the sky with stars.
Now I leap through—
what shattering!

**Dogen**
(1200–1253)

## On *zazen* practice

The moon
abiding in the midst of
serene mind;
billows break
into light.

**Dogen**
(1200–1253)

寂靜

## Mountain dwelling

Things of the past are already long gone
and things to be, distant beyond imagining.
The Tao is just this moment, these words:
plum blossoms fallen; gardenia just opening.

**Ch'ing Kung**
(d.1352)

For all these years, my certain Zen:
neither I nor the world exist.
The *sutras* neat within the box,
my cane hooked upon the wall,
I lie at peace in moonlight
or, hearing water splashing on the rock,
sit up: none can purchase pleasure such as this:
spangled across the step-moss, a million coins!

**Shutaku**
(1308–1388)

Every day, priests minutely examine the Dharma
and endlessly chant complicated *sutras*.
Before doing that, though, they should learn
how to read the love letters sent by the wind and rain,
the snow and moon.

**Ikkyu**
(1394–1481)

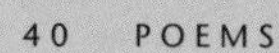

Stilted koans and convoluted answers are all monks have,
pandering endlessly to officials and rich patrons.
Good friends of the Dharma, so proud, let me tell you,
a brothel girl in gold brocade is worth more than any of you.

**Ikkyu**
(1394–1481)

The myriad differences resolved by sitting, all doors opened.
In this still place I follow my nature, be what it may.
From the one hundred flowers I wander freely,
the soaring cliff—my hall of meditation
(with the moon emerged, my mind is motionless).
Sitting on this frosty seat, no further dream of fame.
The forest, the mountain follow their ancient ways,
and through the long spring day, not even the shadow of a bird.

**Reizan**
(d.1411)

Serving the Shogun in the capital,
stained by worldly dust, I found no peace.
Now, straw hat pulled down, I follow the river:
how fresh the sight of gulls across the sand!

**Kodo**
(1370–1433)

## Four haiku by Basho

Autumn—
even the birds
and clouds look old.

Year's end,
all corners
of this floating world, swept.

Cormorant fishing:
how stirring,
how saddening.

Not last night,
not this morning;
melon flowers bloomed.

**Basho**
(1644–1694)

Leaf
of the yam—
raindrop's world.

**Kikaku**
(1661–1707)

In the well bucket,
a morning glory—
I borrow water.

**Lady Chiyo-Jo**
(1701–1775)

A sudden chill—
in our room my dead wife's
comb, underfoot.

**Buson**
(1715–1783)

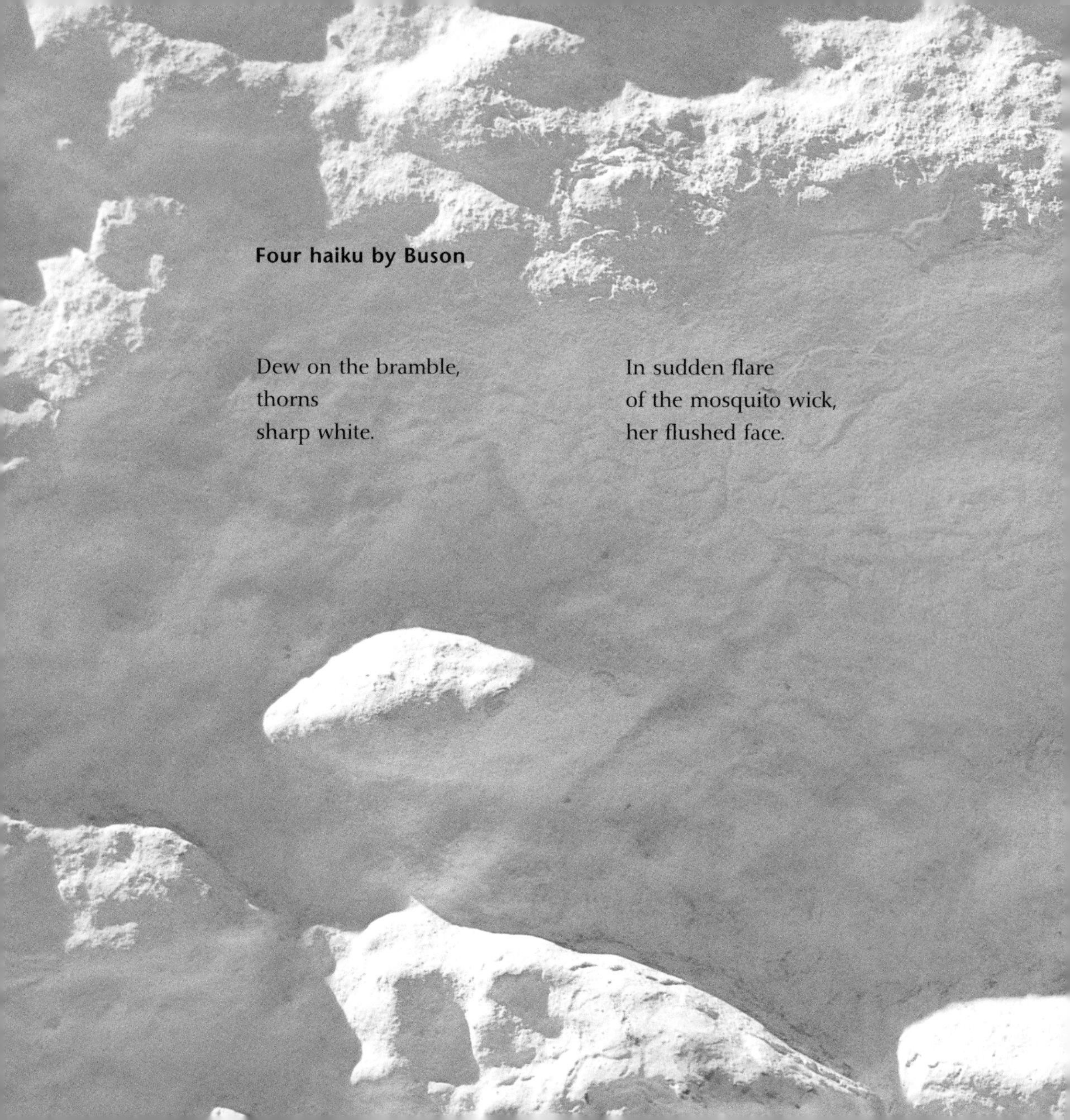

## Four haiku by Buson

Dew on the bramble,
thorns
sharp white.

In sudden flare
of the mosquito wick,
her flushed face.

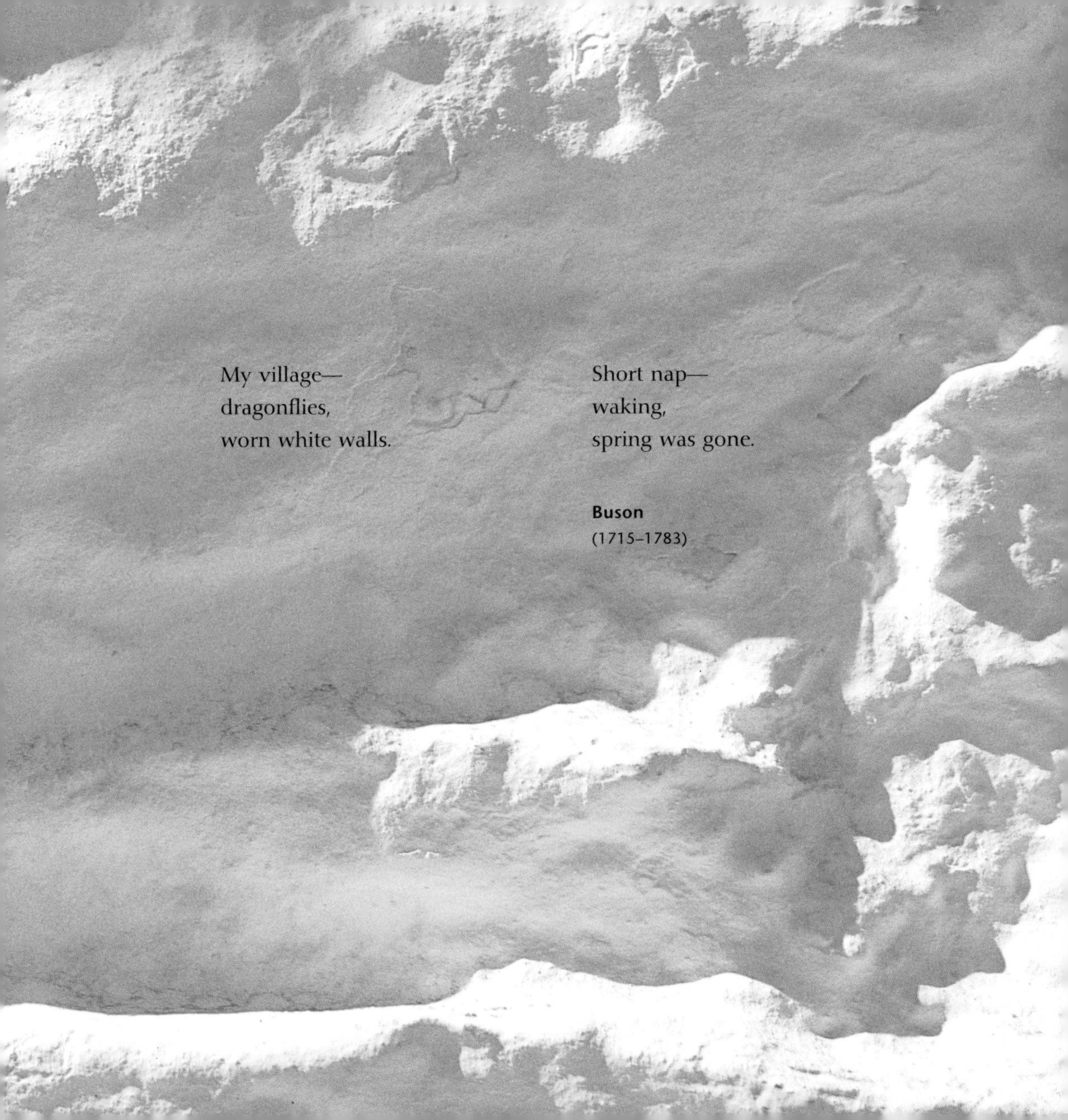

My village—
dragonflies,
worn white walls.

Short nap—
waking,
spring was gone.

**Buson**
(1715–1783)

One sneeze—
skylark's
out of sight.

**Yayu**
(1701–1783)

Nightingale,
rarely seen,
came twice today.

**Kito**
(1740–1789)

Cloud above lotus—
it too
becomes a Buddha.

**Boryu**
(18th century)

## In praise of *zazen*

Sentient beings are in essence Buddhas.
It is like water and ice.
There is no ice without water,
there are no Buddhas outside sentient beings.

What a shame, sentient beings seek afar,
not knowing what is at hand.
It is like wailing from thirst
in the midst of water,
or wandering lost among the poor,
although born a rich man's child.

The cause of rebirth in the six realms
is the darkness of our delusion.
Treading dark path after dark path
when can we escape birth and death?

Mahayana Zen meditation goes beyond all praise.
Giving, keeping precepts, and the other perfections,
chanting Buddha's name, repentance, training and
many other kinds of wholesome deeds
all find their source in *zazen*.

When you sit even once,
the merit obliterates countless wrongdoings.
How can there be evil realms?
The Pure Land is not far.

If by good fortune you have the occasion
to hear this teaching,
admire it and rejoice in it.

You will attain boundless happiness—
how much more if you dedicate yourself
and realize your own nature directly.

This own-nature is no nature.
You are already apart from useless discussions.
The gate opens where cause and effect are inseparable,
the road of not-two, not-three goes straight ahead.

Make the form formless form,
going and returning, not anywhere else.
Make the thought thoughtless thought,
singing and dancing, the Dharma voice.

How vast the sky of unobstructed concentration!
How brilliant the full moon of fourfold wisdom!

At this very moment, what can be sought?
Nirvana is immediate.
This place is the lotus land.
This body is the Buddha body.

**Hakuin**
(1685–1769)

In this world of dreams,
drifting off still more;
and once again speaking
and dreaming of dreams.
Just let it be.

**Ryokan**
(1757–1831)

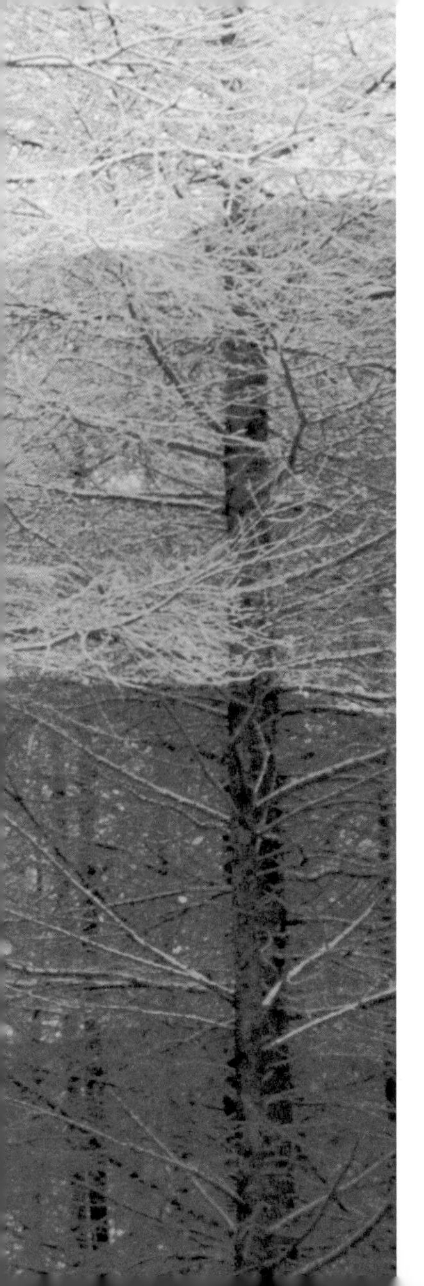

In winter
the seven stars
walk upon a crystal forest.

**Soen Nakagawa**
(1907–1984)

Sound of mountain
sound of ocean
everywhere spring rain.

**Soen Nakagawa**
(1907–1984)

## Shell

Nothing, nothing at all
  is born,
dies, the shell says again
  and again
from the depth of hollowness.
  Its body
swept off by tide—so what?
  It sleeps
in sand, drying in sunlight,
  bathing
in moonlight. Nothing to do
  with sea
or anything else. Over
  and over
it vanishes with the wave.

**Shinkichi Takahashi**
(1901–1987)

Be soft in your practice. Think of the method as a fine silvery stream, not a raging waterfall. Follow the stream, have faith in its course. It will go its own way, meandering here, trickling there. It will find the grooves, the cracks, the crevices. Just follow it. Never let it out of your sight. It will take you.

**Sheng-yen**
(b.1931)

公案

# THE GATELESS GATE

# 1

# Joshu's "mu"

A monk once asked Master Joshu, "Has a dog the Buddha Nature or not?" Joshu said, "Mu!"

**Mumon's commentary**

In studying Zen, one must pass the barriers set up by ancient Zen Masters. For the attainment of incomparable *satori*, one has to cast away his discriminating mind. Those who have not passed the barrier and have not cast away the discriminating mind are all phantoms haunting trees and plants.

Now, tell me, what is the barrier of the Zen Masters? Just this "Mu"–it is the barrier of Zen. It is thus called "the gateless barrier of Zen." Those who have passed the barrier will not only see Joshu clearly, but will go hand in hand with all the Masters of the past, see them face to face. You will see with the same eye that they see with and hear with the same ear. Wouldn't it be wonderful? Don't you want to pass the barrier? Then concentrate yourself into this "Mu," with your 360 bones and 84,000 pores, making your whole body one great inquiry. Day and night, work intently at it. Do not attempt nihilistic or dualistic interpretations. It is like having bolted a red hot iron ball. You try to vomit it but cannot.

Cast away your illusory discriminating knowledge and consciousness accumulated up to now, and keep on working harder. After a while, when your efforts come to fruition, all the oppositions (such as in and out) will naturally be identified. You will then be like a dumb person who has had a wonderful dream: he only knows it personally, within himself. Suddenly you break through the barrier; you will astonish heaven and shake the earth.

It is as if you have snatched the great sword of General Kan. You kill the Buddha if you meet him; you kill the ancient Masters if you meet them. On the brink of life and death you are utterly free, and in the six realms and the four modes of life you live, with great joy, a genuine life in complete freedom.

Now, how should one strive? With might and main work at this "Mu," and *be* "Mu." If you do not waver in your striving, then behold, when the Dharma candle is lighted, darkness is at once enlightened.

**Mumon's poem**

*The dog! The Buddha Nature!*
*The Truth is manifested in full.*
*A moment of yes-and-no:*
*lost are your body and soul.*

## 2

# Hyakujo and a fox

Whenever Master Hyakujo gave *teisho* on Zen, an old man sat with the monks to listen and always withdrew when they did. One day, however, he remained behind, and the Master asked, "Who are you standing here before me?" The old man replied, "I am not a human being. In the past, in the time of the Kasho Buddha, I was the head of this monastery. Once a monk asked me, 'Does an enlightened man also fall into causation or not?' I replied, 'He does not.' Because of this answer, I was made to live as a fox for five hundred lives. Now I beg you, please say the turning words on my behalf and release me from the fox body." The old man then asked Hyakujo, "Does an enlightened man also fall into causation or not?" The Master said, "He does not ignore causation." Hearing this the old man was at once enlightened. Making a bow to Hyakujo he said, "I have now been released from the fox body, which will be found behind the mountain. I dare to make a request of the Master. Please bury it as you would a deceased monk."

The Master had the Ino strike the gavel and announce to the monks that there would be a funeral for a deceased monk after the midday meal. The monks wondered, saying, "We are all in good health. There is no sick monk in the Nirvana Hall. What is it all about?"

After the meal the Master led the monks to a rock behind the mountain, poked out a dead fox with his staff, and cremated it.

In the evening the Master ascended the rostrum in the hall and told the monks the whole story. Obaku thereupon asked, "The old man failed to give the correct turning words and was made to live as a fox for five hundred lives, you say; if, however, his answer had not been incorrect each time, what would he have become?" The Master said, "Come closer to me, I'll tell you." Obaku then stepped forward to Hyakujo and slapped him. The Master laughed aloud, clapping his hands, and said, "I thought a foreigner's beard is red, but I see that it is a foreigner with a red beard."

**Mumon's commentary**

"Not falling into causation." Why was he turned into a fox? "Not ignoring causation." Why was he released from the fox body? If you have an eye to see through this, then you will know that the former head of the monastery did enjoy his five hundred happy blessed lives as a fox.

**Mumon's poem**

*Not falling, not ignoring:*
*odd and even are on one die.*
*Not ignoring, not falling:*
*hundreds and thousands of regrets!*

3

# Gutei raises a finger

Master Gutei, whenever he was questioned, just stuck up one finger.

At one time he had a young attendant, whom a visitor asked, "What is the Zen your Master is teaching?" The boy also stuck up one finger. Hearing of this, Gutei cut off the boy's finger with a knife. As the boy ran out screaming with pain, Gutei called to him. When the boy turned his head, Gutei stuck up his finger. The boy was suddenly enlightened.

When Gutei was about to die, he said to the assembled monks, "I attained Tenryu's Zen of One Finger. I used it all through my life, but could not exhaust it." When he had finished saying this, he died.

### Mumon's commentary

The *satori* of Gutei and of the boy attendant are not in the finger. If you really see through this, Tenryu, Gutei, the boy, and you yourself are all run through with one skewer.

### Mumon's poem

*Gutei made a fool of old Tenryu,*
*with a sharp knife he chastised the boy.*
*Korei raised his hand with no effort,*
*and lo! The great ridge of Mount Ka was split in two!*

## 4

# The foreigner has no beard

Wakuan said, "Why has the foreigner from the West no beard?"

### Mumon's commentary

Training in Zen has to be real training. *Satori* has to be real *satori*. You have to see this foreigner here clearly yourself; then you actually know him. If, however, you talk about "clearly seeing," you have already fallen into dichotomy.

### Mumon's poem

*In front of a fool*
*talk of no dream.*
*The foreigner has no beard:*
*it is adding stupidity to clarity.*

5

# Kyogen's man up a tree

Master Kyogen said, "It is like a man up a tree who hangs from a branch by his mouth; his hands cannot grasp a bough, his feet cannot touch the tree. Another man comes under the tree and asks him the meaning of Bodhidharma's coming from the West. If he does not answer, he does not meet the questioner's need. If he answers, he will lose his life. At such a time, how should he answer?"

**Mumon's commentary**

Even though your eloquence flows like a river, it is all to no avail. Even if you can expound the Great Tripitaka, it is also of no use. If you can really answer it, you will revive the dead and kill the living. If, however, you are unable to answer, wait for Maitreya to come and ask him.

**Mumon's poem**

*Kyogen is just gibbering;*
*how vicious his poison is!*
*Stopping up the monks' mouths,*
*he makes their devil's eyes glare!*

6

## Sakyamuni holds up a flower

Long ago when the World-Honored One was at Mount Grdhrakuta to give a talk, he held up a flower before the assemblage. At this all remained silent. The Venerable Kasho alone broke into a smile. The World-Honored One said, "I have the all-pervading True Dharma, incomparable Nirvana, exquisite teaching of formless form. It does not rely on letters and is transmitted outside scriptures. I now hand it to Maha Kasho."

### Mumon's commentary

Yellow-faced Gotama is certainly outrageous. He turns the noble into the lowly, sells dog-flesh advertised as sheep's head. I thought there was something interesting in it. However at that time if everyone in the assemblage had smiled, to whom would the True Dharma have been handed? Or again, if Kasho had not smiled, would the True Dharma have been transmitted? If you say that the True Dharma can be transmitted, the yellow-faced old man with his loud voice deceived simple villagers. If you say that it cannot be transmitted, then why was Kasho alone approved?

### Mumon's poem

*A flower is held up,*
*and the secret has been revealed.*
*Kasho breaks into a smile;*
*the whole assemblage is at a loss.*

7

# Joshu says "Wash your bowls"

Once a monk made a request of Joshu. "I have just entered the monastery," he said. "Please give me instructions, Master." Joshu said, "Have you had your breakfast?" "Yes, I have," replied the monk. "Then," said Joshu, "wash your bowls." The monk had an insight.

### Mumon's commentary

Joshu opened his mouth and showed his gallbladder, and revealed his heart and liver. If this monk, hearing it, failed to grasp the Truth, he would mistake a bell for a pot.

### Mumon's poem

*Because it is so very clear,*
*it takes longer to come to the realization.*
*If you know at once candlelight is fire,*
*the meal has long been cooked.*

8

## Keichu makes carts

Master Gettan said to a monk: "Keichu made a cart whose wheels had a hundred spokes. Take both front and rear parts away and remove the axle: then what will it be?"

### Mumon's commentary

If you can immediately see through this, your eye will be like a shooting star and your spirituality like lightning.

### Mumon's poem

*When the vividly working wheel turns*
*even an expert is lost.*
*Four directions, above and below:*
*south, north, east, and west.*

## 9

# Daitsu Chisho

Once a monk said to Master Seijo of Koyo, "Daitsu Chisho Buddha did *zazen* on a *bodhi* seat for ten *kalpas*. Buddha Dharma was not manifested, nor did he attain Buddhahood. Why was it?" Jo said, "Your question is splendid indeed." The monk persisted, "He did practice *zazen* on a *bodhi* seat. Why did he not attain Buddhahood?" Jo replied, "Because he did not attain Buddhahood."

### Mumon's commentary

The old foreigner may know it, but he cannot really grasp it. An ordinary man, if he knows it, is a sage. A sage, if he grasps it, is an ordinary man.

### Mumon's poem

*Rather than give the body relief, give relief to the mind:*
*when the mind is at peace, the body is not distressed.*
*If mind and body are both set free,*
*why must the holy saint become a lord?*

# 10

# Seizei, a poor monk

A monk once said to Master Sozan, "I am poor and destitute. I beg you, O Master, please help me and make me rich." Sozan said, "Venerable Seizei!" "Yes, Master," replied Seizei. Sozan remarked, "Having tasted three cups of the best wine of Seigen, do you still say that your lips are not yet moistened?"

**Mumon's commentary**

Seizei assumed a condescending attitude. What is his intention? Sozan has a penetrating eye and has seen through Seizei's mind. Be that as it may, just tell me how the Venerable Seizei could have drunk the wine.

**Mumon's poem**

*His poverty is like Hantan's,*
*his spirit like that of Kou.*
*With no way of earning a livelihood,*
*he dares to compete with the richest of men.*

## 11

# Joshu sees the true nature of two hermits

Joshu came to a hermit and asked, "Are you in? Are you in?" The hermit held up his fist. "The water is too shallow to anchor a vessel," said Joshu, and went away. He then came to another hermit and called out, "Are you in? Are you in?" This hermit also held up his fist. "You are free either to give or to take away, either to kill or to give life," said Joshu, bowing to him.

### Mumon's commentary

Both held up their fists. Why did he approve the one and disapprove the other? Tell me, where is the core of the complication? If you can give a turning word on the point, you will see that Joshu is unrestrained in saying what he wants to say and utterly free either to help the one rise up or to push the other down. Be that as it may, do you know that it was Joshu, on the contrary, whose true nature was seen by the two hermits? If you say the one hermit is superior to the other, you have not yet got the Zen eye. Or if you say there is no difference between the two, you have not yet got the Zen eye, either.

### Mumon's poem

*His eye is a shooting star,*
*his spirit is lightning.*
*A sword to kill,*
*a sword to give life.*

# 12

## Zuigan calls "Master"

Every day Master Zuigan Shigen used to call out to himself, "Oh, Master!" and would answer himself, "Yes?" "Are you awake?" he would ask, and would answer, "Yes, I am." "Never be deceived by others, any day, any time." "No, I will not."

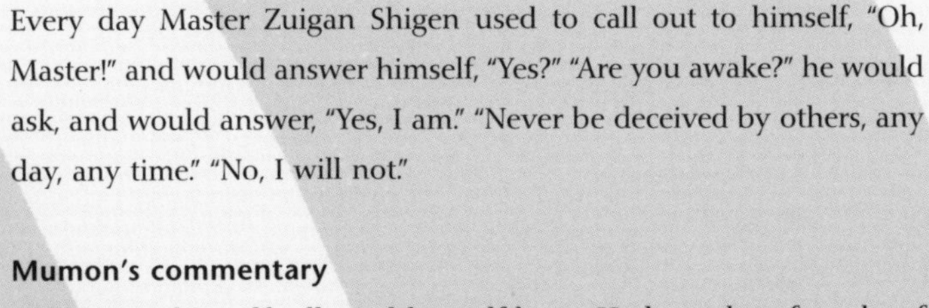

### Mumon's commentary

Old Zuigan himself sells and himself buys. He has a lot of masks of goblins and demons to play with. Why? *Nii*! A calling one, an answering one, an awake one, and one who will not be deceived by others. If you take these different appearances as really existing, you are altogether mistaken. If, however, you would imitate Zuigan, your understanding is that of a fox.

### Mumon's poem

*Those who search for the Way do not realize the Truth,*
*they only know their old discriminating consciousness.*
*This is the cause of the endless cycle of birth and death,*
*yet ignorant people take it for the Original Man*

## 13

# Tokusan carried his bowls

Tokusan one day came down to the dining room carrying his bowls. Seppo said, "Old Master, the bell has not rung and the drum has not yet been struck. Where are you going with your bowls?" Tokusan at once turned back to his room. Seppo told this incident to Ganto, who remarked, "Great Master though he is, Tokusan has not yet grasped the last word of Zen." Hearing of it, Tokusan sent his attendant to call Ganto in, and asked, "Do you not approve of me?" Ganto whispered his reply to him. Tokusan was satisfied and silent. The next day Tokusan appeared on the rostrum. Sure enough, his talk was different from the usual ones. Ganto came in front of the monastery, laughed heartily, clapping his hands, and said, "What a great joy it is! The old Master has now grasped the last word of Zen. From now on nobody in the world can ever make light of him."

### Mumon's commentary

As for the last word of Zen, neither Ganto nor Tokusan has ever heard of it, even in a dream. If I examine it carefully, they are like puppets set on a shelf.

### Mumon's poem

*If you understand the first word of Zen*
*you will know the last word.*
*The last word or the first word–*
*"it" is not a word.*

14

# Nansen kills a cat

Once the monks of the Eastern Hall and the Western Hall were disputing about a cat. Nansen, holding up the cat, said, "Monks, if you can say a word of Zen, I will spare the cat. If you cannot, I will kill it!" No monk could answer. Nansen finally killed the cat. In the evening, when Joshu came back, Nansen told him of the incident. Joshu took off his sandal, put it on his head, and walked off. Nansen said, "If you had been there, I could have saved the cat!"

**Mumon's commentary**

You tell me, what is the real meaning of Joshu's putting his sandal on his head? If you can give the turning words on this point, you will see that Nansen's action was not in vain. If you cannot, beware!

**Mumon's poem**

*Had Joshu only been there,*
*he would have taken action.*
*Had he snatched the sword away,*
*Nansen would have begged for his life.*

## 15

# Tozan gets sixty blows

When Tozan came to have an interview with Unmon, Unmon asked, "Where have you been recently?" "At Sado, Master," Tozan replied. "Where did you stay during the last *ge*-period?" "At Hozu of Konan," replied Tozan. "When did you leave there?" "On the twenty-fifth of August," Tozan answered. Unmon exclaimed, "I give you sixty blows with my stick!" The next day Tozan came up again and asked the Master, "Yesterday you gave me sixty blows with your stick. I do not know where my fault was." Unmon cried out, "You rice-bag! Have you been prowling about like that from Kosei to Konan?" At this Tozan was enlightened.

**Mumon's commentary**

If Unmon at that time, by giving Tozan the fodder of the Truth, had awakened him to the vivid, dynamic Zen life, Unmon's school would not have declined. In the sea of yes-and-no, Tozan struggled all through the night. When the day broke and he came to see the Master again, Unmon helped him break through. Though Tozan was immediately enlightened, he was not bright enough. Let me ask you, "Should Tozan be beaten, or not?" If you say he ought to be beaten, trees and grasses and everything ought to be beaten. If you say he should not be beaten, then Unmon is telling a falsehood. If you can be clear on this point, you and Tozan will breathe together.

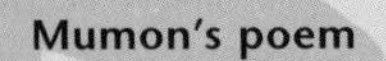

### Mumon's poem

*A lion trains its cubs this way:*
*if they walk ahead, it kicks them and quickly dodges.*
*Against his will, Tozan had to be struck again;*
*the first arrow only nicked him, but the second went deep.*

# 16

## Bell-sound and priest's robe

Unmon said, "Look! This world is vast and wide. Why do you put on your priest's robe at the sound of the bell?"

### Mumon's commentary

Now, in studying Zen and disciplining oneself in Zen, one must strictly avoid following sounds and clinging to forms. Even though one may be enlightened by hearing a sound, or have one's mind clarified by seeing a form, this is just a matter of course. It is nothing to talk about, either, if a Zen man is able to master sounds and control forms, and thus can clearly see the reality of everything and is wonderfully free in everything he does. Though it may be so, you tell me, does the sound come to your ear, or does your ear go to the sound? Even if you are able to transcend both sound and silence, how do you speak of that fact? If you listen with your ear, you cannot truly get it. When you hear with your eye, then you can really get it.

### Mumon's poem

*If you understand "it," all things are One;*
*if you do not, they are different and separate.*
*If you do not understand "it," all things are One;*
*if you do, they are different and separate.*

# 17

# The National Teacher calls three times

法

The National Teacher called to his attendant three times, and the attendant answered three times. The National Teacher said, "I thought I had transgressed against you, but you too had transgressed against me."

### Mumon's commentary

The National Teacher called three times, and his tongue dropped to the ground. The attendant answered three times, and softening his light, he gave it out. The National Teacher, as he got old and was feeling lonely, pushed the cow's head down to the grass to feed her. The attendant would not simply accept it. Even delicious food cannot attract a full stomach. Now, tell me, how did they transgress?

When the nation is at peace, men of talent are respected;
when the family is well off, the children maintain their status.

### Mumon's poem

*An iron collar with no hole, he has to wear it.*
*It's no easy matter, the trouble passes on to his descendants.*
*If you want to support the gate and sustain the house,*
*you must climb a mountain of swords with bare feet.*

## 18

# Tozan's three pounds of flax

A monk asked Master Tozan, "What is Buddha?" Tozan said, "Three pounds of flax."

### Mumon's commentary

Old Tozan studied a bit of clam-Zen, and opening the shell a little, revealed his liver and intestines. Though it may be so, tell me, where do you see Tozan?

### Mumon's poem

*Thrust forth is "Three pounds of flax!"*
*Words are intimate, even more so is the mind.*
*He who talks about right and wrong*
*is a man of right and wrong.*

## 19

# Ordinary mind is Tao

Joshu once asked Nansen, "What is Tao?" Nansen answered, "Ordinary mind is Tao." "Then should we direct ourselves toward it or not?" asked Joshu. "If you try to direct yourself toward it, you go away from it," answered Nansen. Joshu continued, "If we do not try, how can we know that it is Tao?" Nansen replied, "Tao does not belong to knowing or to not-knowing. Knowing is illusion; not-knowing is blankness. If you really attain to Tao of no-doubt, it is like the great void, so vast and boundless. How, then, can there be right and wrong in the Tao?" At these words, Joshu was suddenly enlightened.

**Mumon's commentary**

Questioned by Joshu, Nansen immediately shows that the tile is disintegrating, the ice is dissolving, and no communication whatsoever is possible. Even though Joshu may be enlightened, he can truly get it only after studying for thirty more years.

**Mumon's poem**

*Hundreds of flowers in spring, the moon in autumn,*
*a cool breeze in summer, and snow in winter;*
*if there is no vain cloud in your mind*
*for you it is a good season.*

20

# The man of great strength

Master Shogen said, "Why is it that a man of great strength cannot lift his leg?" Again he said, "It is not with his tongue that he speaks."

### Mumon's commentary

Of Shogen it must be said that he emptied his intestines and turned his belly out. Yet no one understands it. Even though there is a man who immediately understands it, I will give him severe blows with my stick if he comes to me. Why? *Nii*! If you want to know pure gold, see it in the midst of fire.

### Mumon's poem

*Lifting his leg he kicks up the Scented Ocean,*
*lowering his head he looks down on the Four Dhyana Heavens.*
*There is no place to put this gigantic body.*
*You please add another line.*

## 21

# Unmon's shit-stick

A monk asked Unmon, "What is Buddha?" Unmon said, "A shit-stick!" (*Kan-shiketsu!*)

### Mumon's commentary

Of Unmon it must be said that he is so poor that he cannot prepare even plain food; he is so busy that he cannot write properly. Very likely they may bring out the shit-stick to support the gate. The outcome is just obvious.

### Mumon's poem

*A flash of lightning!*
*Sparks struck from a flint!*
*If you blink your eye*
*it is gone.*

22

# Kasho and a flagpole

Ananda once said to Kasho, "The World-Honored One transmitted to you the brocade robe. What else did he transmit to you?" Kasho called out, "Ananda!" Ananda answered, "Yes, sir." Kasho said, "Pull down the flagpole at the gate."

**Mumon's commentary**

If you can give the exact turning word to this koan, you will see that the meeting at Mount Grdhrakuta is definitely present here. If not, then know that Vipasyin Buddha is still unable to get the Truth even though he began his seeking in remote antiquity.

**Mumon's poem**

*The calling out is good, but even better the answering.*
*How many are there who have opened their true eyes?*
*The elder brother calling out, the younger brother replying,*
*the family shame is revealed.*
*This is the spring that does not belong to Yin and Yang.*

## 23

# Think neither good nor evil

The Sixth Patriarch was once pursued by the monk Myo to Daiyurei. The Patriarch, seeing Myo coming, laid the robe and bowl on a stone, and said, "This robe symbolizes faith; how can it be fought for by force? I will leave it to you to take it." Myo tried to take up the robe, but it was as immovable as a mountain. Myo was terrified and hesitated. He said, "I have come for Dharma, not for the robe. I beg you, please teach me, O lay brother!" The Sixth Patriarch said, "Think neither good nor evil. At such a moment, what is the True Self of Monk Myo?" At this, Myo was at once enlightened. His whole body was dripping with sweat. With tears he made a bow and asked, "Beside these secret words and meanings, is there any further significance or not?" The Patriarch said, "What I have just told you is not secret. If you will realize your True Self, what is secret is in you-yourself." Myo said,

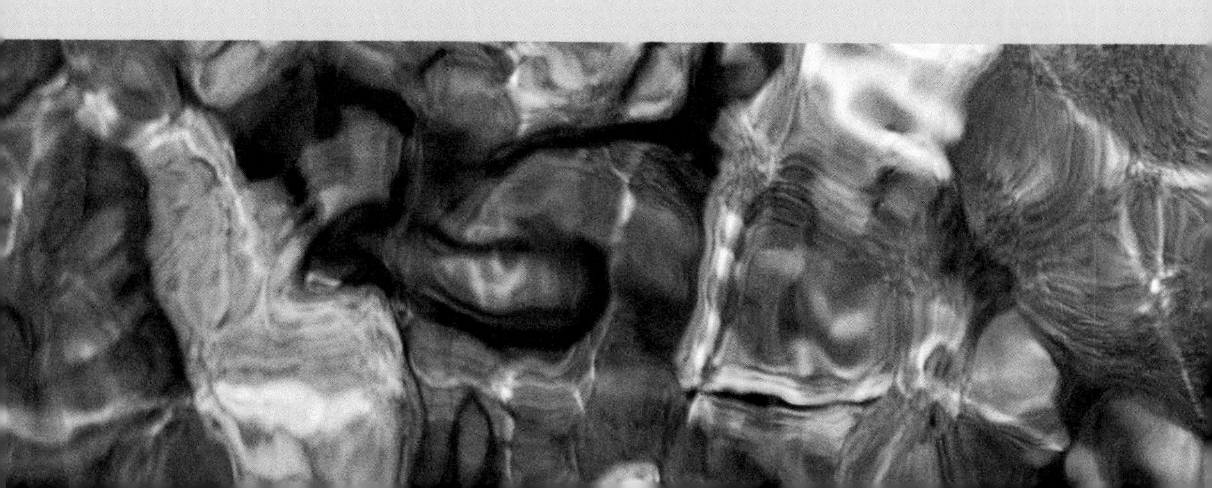

"Although at Obai I followed other monks in training, I did not awaken to my True Self. Thanks to your instruction, which is to the point, I am like one who has drunk water and actually experienced himself whether it is cold or warm. You are really my teacher, lay brother!" The Patriarch said, "if you are so awakened, both you and I have Obai as our teacher. Live up to your attainment with care."

**Mumon's commentary**

Of the Sixth Patriarch it has to be said that in an emergency he did something extraordinary. He has a grandmotherly kindness; it is as if he had peeled a fresh litchi, removed its seed, and then put it into your mouth so that you need only swallow it.

**Mumon's poem**

*You may describe it, but in vain, picture it,*
*but to no avail.*
*You can never praise it full: stop all your groping*
*and maneuvering.*
*There is nowhere to hide the True Self.*
*When the world collapses, "it" is indestructible.*

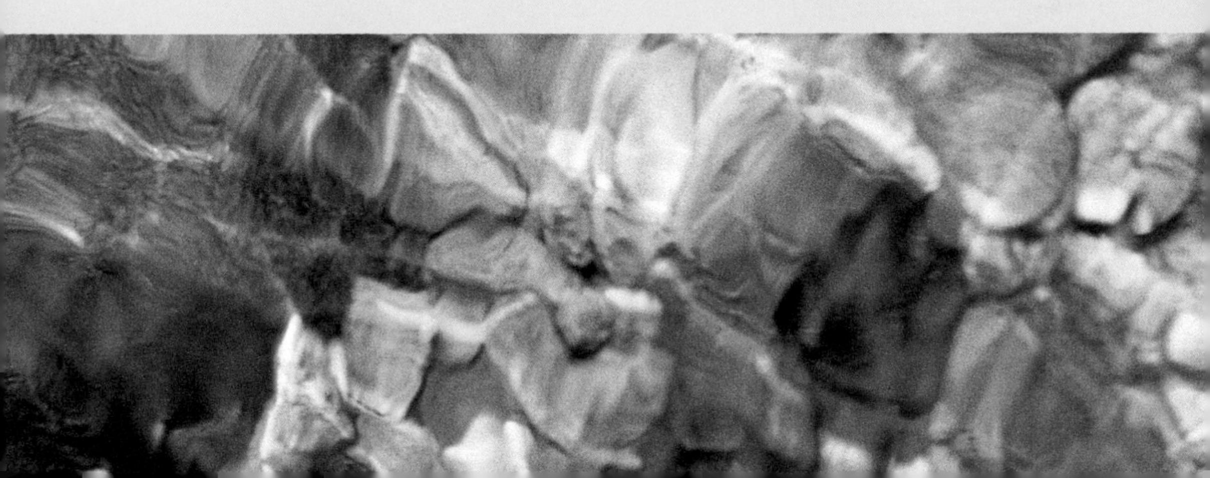

# 24

## Abandon words and speaking

A monk once asked Master Fuketsu, "Both speaking and silence are concerned with *ri-bi* relativity. How can we be free and nontransgressing?" Fuketsu said,

"How fondly I remember Konan in March!
The partridges are calling, and the flowers are fragrant."

**Mumon's commentary**

Fuketsu's Zen works like lightning. He has his way and marches along. But why does he rely on the tongue of the ancient poet and does not get rid of it? If you can clearly see into this point, you may attain absolute freedom. Abandon words and speaking, and say a word!

**Mumon's poem**

*He used no high-flown words;*
*before the mouth is opened, "it" is revealed.*
*If you keep on chattering glibly,*
*know you will never get "it."*

## 25

# Talk by the monk of the third seat

Master Gyozan had a dream. He went to Maitreya's place and was given the third seat. A venerable monk there struck the table with a gavel and announced, "Today the talk will be given by the monk of the third seat." Gyozan struck the table with the gavel and said, "The Dharma of Mahayana goes beyond the Four Propositions and transcends the One Hundred Negations. Listen carefully!"

### Mumon's commentary

Tell me, did he give a talk or did he not? If you open your mouth, you will lose "it." If you shut your mouth, you will also miss "it". Even if you neither open nor shut your mouth, you are a hundred and eight thousand miles away.

### Mumon's poem

*Broad daylight under the blue sky!*
*In a dream he talks of a dream.*
*Humbug! Humbug!*
*He deceived the whole audience.*

## 26

# Two monks rolled up the bamboo blinds

The monks gathered in the hall to hear the Great Hogen of Seiryo give *teisho* before the midday meal. Hogen pointed to the bamboo blinds. At this two monks went to the blinds, and rolled them up alike. Hogan said, "One has it; the other has not."

### Mumon's commentary

Tell me, which one has it and which one has not? If you have your Zen eye opened at this point, you will then know how Master Seiryo failed. Be that as it may, you are strictly warned against arguing about "has" and "has not."

### Mumon's poem

*When they are rolled up, bright and clear is the great emptiness.*
*The great emptiness does not yet come up to our teaching.*
*Why don't you cast away emptiness and everything?*
*Then it is so lucid and perfect that even the wind does not pass through.*

# 27

## Neither mind nor Buddha

A monk once asked Master Nansen, "Is there any Dharma that has not yet been taught to the people?" Nansen said, "Yes, there is." The monk asked, "What is the Dharma that has not been taught to the people?" Nansen said, "It is neither mind, nor Buddha, nor beings."

**Mumon's commentary**

Nansen, being asked the question, had to use up all his resources at once. How feeble and awkward!

**Mumon's poem**

*Too much courtesy impairs your virtue;*
*silence is certainly effective.*
*Let it be so. Even if the blue ocean should change,*
*"it" will never be communicated to you.*

28

# Well-known Ryutan

Tokusan once called on Ryutan to ask for instruction and stayed until night fell. Ryutan said, "It is getting late; you had better leave." At last Tokusan said good-bye, lifted up the door curtain, and went out. Noticing that it was dark, he turned back and said, "It is dark outside." Ryutan thereupon lit a candle and handed it to him. Tokusan was about to take it when Ryutan blew it out. At this Tokusan was all of a sudden enlightened. He made a bow. Ryutan asked, "What realization do you have?" Tokusan replied, "From now on I will not doubt the sayings of any of the great Zen Masters in the world."

The next day Ryutan mounted the rostrum and declared, "Among the monks here there is a fellow whose fangs are like swords, and whose mouth is like a bowl of blood. You may strike him with a stick but he will not turn his head. Some day in the future, he will establish his way on a steep and lofty peak."

Tokusan then took out his notes and commentaries on the *Diamond Sutra*, and in front of the monastery hall he held up a burning torch and said, "Even though one masters various profound philosophies, it is like placing a single strand of hair in the great sky; even if one gains all the essential knowledge in the world, it is like throwing a drop of water into a deep ravine." Taking up his notes and commentaries, he burned them all. Then he left with gratitude.

### Mumon's commentary

When Tokusan had not yet left his home, his mind was indignant and his tongue sharp. He confidently came to the south in order to exterminate the "special transmission outside scriptures." When he reached the road to Reishu, he talked to an old woman who sold *tenjin*. The old woman said, "Venerable Monk, what books do you carry in your box?" Tokusan said, "They are notes and commentaries on the *Diamond Sutra*." The old woman said, "It is said in the *sutra* that 'the past mind is unattainable; the present mind is unattainable; the future mind is unattainable.' Which mind, Venerable Monk, are you going to light up?" Tokusan was unable to answer this question and had to shut his mouth tight. Even so, he could not die the Great Death at the old woman's words, and finally asked, "Is there a Zen Master in the neighborhood?" The old woman replied, "Master Ryutan lives five miles away." Arriving at Ryutan's monastery, he was completely defeated. It has to be said that his former words and his latter words do not agree. Ryutan is like the mother who, because she loves her child too much, does not realize how meddlesome she herself is. Finding a little piece of live coal in Tokusan, he quickly poured muddy water over him. Looking at it calmly, I would say that the whole story is just a farce.

### Mumon's poem

*Far better seeing the face than hearing the name;*
*far better hearing the name than seeing the face.*
*Though he saved his nose,*
*alas, he has lost his eyes!*

## 29

# Neither the wind nor the flag

The wind was flapping a temple flag. Two monks were arguing about it. One said the flag was moving; the other said the wind was moving. Arguing back and forth they could come to no agreement. The Sixth Patriarch said, "It is neither the wind nor the flag that is moving. It is your mind that is moving." The two monks were struck with awe.

### Mumon's commentary

It is neither the wind nor the flag nor the mind that is moving. Where do you see the heart of the Patriarch? If you can see clearly, you will know that the two monks obtained gold intending to buy iron. Also you will know that the Patriarch could not repress his compassion and made an awkward scene.

### Mumon's poem

*The wind moves, the flag moves, the mind moves:*
*all of them missed it.*
*Though he knows how to open his mouth,*
*he does not see he was caught by words.*

## 30

# Mind is Buddha

Taibai once asked Baso, "What is Buddha?" Baso answered, "Mind is Buddha."

**Mumon's commentary**

If you can at once grasp "it," you are wearing Buddha clothes, eating Buddha food, speaking Buddha words, and living Buddha life; you are a Buddha yourself. Though this may be so, Taibai has misled a number of people and let them trust a scale with a stuck pointer. Don't you know that one has to rinse out his mouth for three days if he has uttered the word "Buddha"? If he is a real Zen man, he will stop his ears and rush away when he hears "Mind is Buddha."

**Mumon's poem**

*A fine day under the blue sky!*
*Don't foolishly look here and there.*
*If you still ask "What is Buddha?"*
*it is like pleading your innocence while clutching stolen goods.*

## 31

# Joshu saw through the old woman

A monk asked an old woman, "Which way should I take to Mount Gotai?" The old woman said, "Go straight on!" When the monk had taken a few steps, she remarked, "He may look like a fine monk, but he too goes off like that!" Later a monk told Joshu about it. Joshu said, "Wait a while. I will go and see through that old woman for you." The next day off he went, and asked her the same question. The old woman gave him the same reply. When he returned, Joshu announced to the monks, "I have seen through the old woman of Mount Gotai for you."

### Mumon's commentary

The old woman knew how to work out a strategy and win the victory while sitting in her tent. Yet she is not aware of the bandit stealing into the tent. Old Joshu is skillful enough to creep into the enemy's camp and menace their fortress. Yet he does not look like a grown-up. Upon close examination, they are both at fault. Now tell me, how did Joshu see through the old woman?

### Mumon's poem

*The question is the same each time,*
*the answer, too, is the same.*
*In the rice there is sand,*
*in the mud there are thorns.*

# 32

## A non-Buddhist questions the Buddha

A non-Buddhist once asked the World-Honored One, "I do not ask for words, nor do I ask for no-words." The World-Honored One remained seated. The non-Buddhist praised him, saying, "The great compassion of the World-Honored One has dispelled the clouds of my ignorance and enabled me to be enlightened." Making a bow of gratitude, he departed. Ananda then asked Buddha, "What realization did the non-Buddhist have that made him praise you like that?" The World-Honored One replied, "He is like a high-mettled horse which starts at even the shadow of the whip."

**Mumon's commentary**

Ananda is Buddha's disciple, yet his understanding falls far short of the non-Buddhist's. Now tell me, how different are they, the Buddha's disciple and the non-Buddhist?

**Mumon's poem,**

*He walks along the edge of a sword*
*and runs over the sharp ridges of an ice floe.*
*You need take no steps,*
*let go your hold on the cliff!*

33

# No mind, no Buddha

A monk once asked Baso, "What is Buddha?" Baso answered, "No mind, no Buddha."

### Mumon's commentary

If you can see into it here, your Zen study has been completed.

### Mumon's poem

*If you meet a swordsman in the street, give him a sword;*
*unless you meet a poet, do not offer a poem.*
*In talking to people, tell them three quarters only,*
*never let them have the other part.*

## 34

# Wisdom is not Tao

Nansen said, "Mind is not Buddha; wisdom is not Tao."

### Mumon's commentary

Of Nansen it has to be said that on getting old he was lost to shame. Just opening his stinking mouth a little, he reveals his family shame. Even so, only a very few feel grateful for it.

### Mumon's poem

*The sky is clear and the sun appears;*
*rain falls and the earth is moistened.*
*Without restraint he has explained everything,*
*yet how few are able to grasp it!*

## 35

# Sen-jo and her soul are separated

Goso asked a monk, "Sen-jo and her soul are separated: which is the true one?"

**Mumon's commentary**

If you are enlightened in the truth of this koan, you will then know that coming out of one husk and getting into another is like a traveler's putting up in hotels. In case you are not yet enlightened, do not rush about blindly. When suddenly earth, water, fire, and air are decomposed, you will be like a crab fallen into boiling water, struggling with its seven arms and eight legs. Do not say then that I have not warned you.

**Mumon's poem**

*Ever the same, the moon among the clouds;*
*different from each other, the mountain and the valley.*
*How wonderful! How blessed!*
*Is this one, or two?*

36

# Meeting a man of Tao on the way

Goso said, "If you meet a man of Tao on the way, greet him neither with words nor with silence. Now tell me, how will you greet him?"

### Mumon's commentary

If you can give an apt answer to the question, it certainly is a matter for congratulation. If you are not yet able to give one, be alert in every aspect of your life.

### Mumon's poem

*If you meet a man of Tao on the way,*
*greet him neither with words nor with silence.*
*I'll give him with my fist the hardest blow I can—*
*get it at once, get it immediately!*

37

# The oak tree in the front garden

A monk once asked Joshu, "What is the meaning of the Patriarch's coming from the West?" Joshu answered, "The oak tree in the front garden."

### Mumon's commentary

If you can firmly grasp the essence of Joshu's answer, for you there is no Sakyamuni in the past and no Maitreya in the future.

### Mumon's poem

*Words do not convey actualities;*
*letters do not embody the spirit of the mind.*
*He who attaches himself to words is lost;*
*he who abides with letters will remain in ignorance.*

# 38

## A buffalo passes through a window

Goso said, "To give an example, it is like a buffalo passing through a window. Its head, horns, and four legs have all passed through. Why is it that its tail cannot?"

### Mumon's commentary

If you can penetrate to the point of this koan, open your Zen eye to it, and give a turning word to it, you will then be able to repay the four obligations above and help the three existences below. If you still cannot do so, work with the tail singleheartedly until you can really grasp it as your own.

### Mumon's poem

*If it passes through, it falls into a ditch;*
*if it turns back, it is destroyed.*
*This tiny tail,*
*how extremely marvelous!*

## 39

# Unmon says "You have missed it!"

A monk once wanted to ask Unmon a question and started to say, "The light serenely shines over the whole universe." Before he had even finished the first line, Unmon suddenly interrupted, "Isn't that the poem of Chosetsu Shusai?" The monk answered, "Yes, it is." Unmon said, "You have missed it!"

Later Master Shishin took up this koan and said, "Now tell me, why has this monk missed it?"

### Mumon's commentary

In this koan, if you can grasp how lofty and unapproachable Unmon's Zen working is, and why the monk missed it, then you can be a teacher in heaven and on earth. In case you are not yet clear about it, you will be unable to save yourself.

### Mumon's poem

*A line is dropped in a swift stream;*
*greedy for the bait, he is caught.*
*If you open your mouth only a little,*
*your life is lost!*

# 40

## Kicking over the pitcher

When Master Isan was studying under Hyakujo, he worked as a *tenzo* at the monastery. Hyakujo wanted to choose an abbot for Daii Monastery. He told the head monk and all the rest of his disciples to make their Zen presentations, and the ablest one would be sent to found the monastery. Then Hyakujo took a pitcher, placed it on the floor, and asked the question: "This must not be called a pitcher. What do you call it?" The head monk said, "It cannot be called a wooden sandal." Hyakujo then asked Isan. Isan walked up, kicked over the pitcher, and left. Hyakujo said, "The head monk has been defeated by Isan." So Isan was ordered to start the monastery.

### Mumon's commentary

Extremely valiant though he is, Isan could not after all jump out of Hyakujo's trap. Upon careful examination, he followed what is heavy, refusing what is light. Why? *Nii!* Taking the towel band from his head, he put on an iron yoke.

### Mumon's poem

*Throwing away bamboo baskets and wooden ladles,*
*with a direct blow he cuts off complications.*
*Hyakujo tries to stop him with his strict barrier, but in vain.*
*The tip of his foot creates innumerable Buddhas.*

## 41

# Bodhidharma and peace of mind

Bodhidharma sat in *zazen* facing the wall. The Second Patriarch, who had been standing in the snow, cut off his arm and said, "Your disciple's mind is not yet at peace. I beg you, my teacher, please give it peace." Bodhidharma said, "Bring the mind to me, and I will set it at rest." The Second Patriarch said, "I have searched for the mind, and it is finally unattainable." Bodhidharma said, "I have thoroughly set it at rest for you."

**Mumon's commentary**

The broken–toothed old foreigner proudly came over–a hundred thousand miles across the sea. This was as if he were raising waves where there was no wind. Toward his end, Bodhidharma could enlighten only one disciple, but even he was crippled. *Ii*! Shasanro does not know even four characters.

**Mumon's poem**

*Coming from the West, and directly pointing–*
*this great affair was caused by the transmission.*
*The trouble-maker who created a stir in Zen circles*
*is, after all, you.*

## 42

# A woman comes out of meditation

Once long long ago, the World-Honored One came to the place where many Buddhas were assembled. When Manjusri arrived there, the Buddhas all returned to their original places. Only a woman remained, close to the Buddha seat in deep meditation. Manjusri spoke to the Buddha, "Why can a woman be close to the Buddha seat, and I cannot?" The Buddha told Manjusri, "You awaken this woman from her meditation and ask her yourself." Manjusri walked around the woman three times, snapped his fingers once, then took her up to the Brahma Heaven and tried all his supernatural powers, but he was unable to bring her out of meditation. The World-Honored One said, "Even hundreds of thousands of Manjusris would be unable to bring her out of meditation. Down below, past one billion, two hundred million countries, as innumerable as the sands of the Ganges, there is a Bodhisattva called Momyo. He will be able to awaken her from meditation." In an instant Momyo emerged from the earth and worshiped the World-Honored One. The World-Honored One gave him the order. Momyo then walked to the woman and snapped his fingers only once. At this the woman came out of her meditation.

### Mumon's commentary

Old Sakya put on a clumsy play and was no better than a child. Now tell me: Manjusri is the teacher of the Seven Buddhas; why could he not bring the woman out of her meditation? Momyo is a Bodhisattva of the initial stage; why could he do so? If you can firmly grasp this point, then for you this busy life of ignorance and discrimination will be the life of supreme *satori.*

### Mumon's poem

*The one could awaken her, the other could not;*
*both are completely free.*
*A god mask and a devil mask,*
*the failure is wonderful indeed.*

# 43

## Shuzan and a staff

Master Shuzan held up his staff, and showing it to the assembled disciples said, "You monks, if you call this a staff, you are committed to the name. If you call it not-a-staff, you negate the fact. Tell me, you monks, what do you call it?"

### Mumon's commentary

If you call it a staff, you are committed to the name. If you call it not-a-staff, you negate the fact. You cannot talk; you cannot be silent. Quick! Speak! Speak! Quick!

### Mumon's poem

*Holding up a staff,*
*he is carrying out the orders to kill and to revive.*
*Where committing and negating are interfusing,*
*Buddhas and Patriarchs have to beg for their lives.*

## 44

# Basho and a stick

Master Basho said to the monks, "If you have a stick, I shall give one to you. If you do not have a stick, I shall take it away from you."

**Mumon's commentary**

It helps you cross the river where the bridge is broken. It accompanies you as you return to the village on a moonless night. If you call it a stick, you will go to hell as fast as an arrow.

**Mumon's poem**

*The deep and the shallow wherever they may be*
*are all in my hand.*
*It sustains heaven and supports the earth,*
*and promotes Zen Truth wherever it may be.*

45

# Who is he?

Our Patriarch Master Hoen of Tozan said, "Sakyamuni and Maitreya are but his servants. Now tell me, who is he?"

**Mumon's commentary**

If you can see him and are absolutely clear about him, it will be like coming upon your own father at the crossroads. You do not have to ask someone else whether you are correct or incorrect in recognizing him as your father.

**Mumon's poem**

*Do not draw another man's bow;*
*do not ride another man's horse;*
*do not defend another man's fault;*
*do not inquire into another man's affairs.*

# 46

## Step forward from the top of a pole

Master Sekiso said, "From the top of a pole one hundred feet high, how do you step forward?" An ancient Master also said that one sitting at the top of a pole one hundred feet high, even if he has attained "it," has not yet been truly enlightened. He must step forward from the top of the pole one hundred feet high and manifest his whole body in the ten directions.

### Mumon's commentary

If you can step forward and turn back, is there anything you dislike as unworthy? But even so, tell me, from the top of a pole one hundred feet high, how do you step forward? *Sah*!

### Mumon's poem

*The eye in the forehead has gone blind,*
*and he has been misled by the stuck pointer on the scale.*
*He has thrown away his body and laid down his life—*
*a blind man is leading other blind men.*

## 47

# Tosotsu's three barriers

Master Juetsu of Tosotsu made three barriers to test monks.

To inquire after the Truth, groping your way through the underbrush, is for the purpose of seeing into your nature. Here, now, where is your nature, Venerable Monk?

If you realize your own nature, you certainly are free from life and death. When your eyes are closed, how can you be free from life and death?

If you are free from life and death, you know where you will go. When the four elements are decomposed, where do you go?

### Mumon's commentary

If you can rightly give the three turning words here, you will be the master wherever you may be, and live up to the Dharma no matter how varied the circumstances. If, however, you are unable to give them, I warn you, you will get tired of the food you have bolted, and well-chewed food keeps hunger away.

### Mumon's poem

*This one instant, as it is, is an infinite number of* kalpas.
*An infinite number of* kalpas *are at the same time this one instant.*
*If you see into this fact,*
*the True Self which is seeing has been seen into.*

# 48

## Kempo's one way

A monk once asked Master Kempo, "The Bhagavats of the ten directions have one way to Nirvana. I wonder where this one way is." Kempo held up his stick, drew a line, and said, "Here it is!"

Later the monk asked Unmon for his instruction on this *mondo*. Unmon held up his fan and said, "This fan has jumped up to the Thirty-third Heaven and hit the nose of the deity there. The carp of the Eastern Sea leaps, and it rains cats and dogs."

### Mumon's commentary

The one goes to the bottom of the deep sea and raises a cloud of sand and dust. The other stands on the top of a towering mountain and raises foaming waves to touch the sky. The one holds, the other lets go, and each, using only one hand, sustains the teachings of Zen. What they do is exactly like two children who come running from opposite directions and crash into each other. In the world there is hardly anyone who has truly awakened. From the absolute point of view, the two great Masters do not really know where the way is.

### Mumon's poem

*Before taking a step you have already arrived.*
*Before moving your tongue you have finished teaching,*
*even if at each step you may be ahead of him,*
*know there is still another way up.*

十牛図頌

# THE OX-HERDING PICTURES

# Search

Vigorously cutting a path through the brambles, you look for the ox;
rivers wide, mountains far, the path gets longer.
Running out of strength, mind exhausted, you cannot find it.
Rustling of maple leaves,
singing of evening cicadas.

## Finding traces

By the water, deep within the forest, you find traces.
Leaving fragrant grasses behind, you study the signs.
Following the tracks, you enter endless mountains.
Distant sky–how can the tip of its nose be hidden elsewhere?

## Seeing

Chirping, a yellow oriole on a branch.
Warm sun, gentle breeze, green willows on the bank.
No place to turn around–
in brambles, its head and horn are not clearly seen.

## Catching

Through tremendous effort you have caught the ox.
Still its will is strong, its body vigorous.
Sometimes it runs to a high ground,
sometimes it disappears deep in mist.

## Taming

You cannot put whip and tether aside
for fear it will wander into a swamp.
Once trained to be gentle,
free of rope the ox follows your way.

## Riding home

Taking a winding path you ride the ox home.
The tune of your rustic flute permeates the evening haze.
Each note, each song: feeling unbounded
knowing the sound is beyond lips and mouth.

## Forgetting it

You have ridden home on the ox.
At rest, you forget it.
Bright sun high in the sky; you daydream blissfully
leaving whip and tether behind in the grass-roof hut.

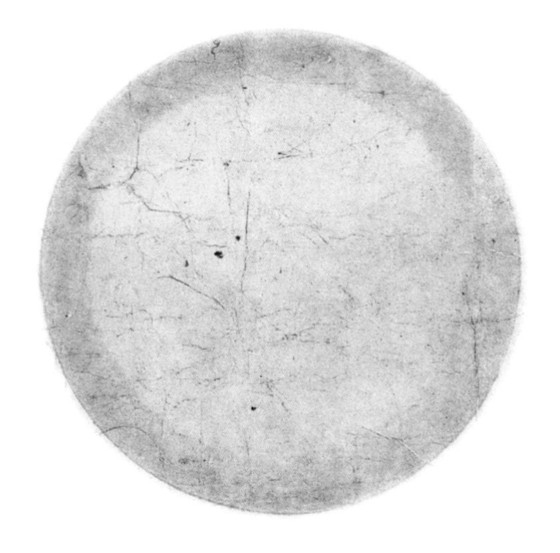

# Forgetting all

Whip and tether, you, the ox all empty.
Vast blue sky cannot be reached by ideas.
How can the fire's flame sustain the snowflakes?
Having reached here, you are in accord with the ancient way.

# Returning to the source

You have returned to the source; effort is over.
The intimate self is blind and deaf.
Inside the hut, nothing outside is seen.
Waters are boundless, flowers red.

# Entering the marketplace with giving hands

You go into the marketplace barefooted, unadorned,
smeared with mud, covered with dust, smiling.
Using no supernatural power
you bring the withered trees to bloom.

# GLOSSARY

**awakened mind** see **enlightenment**

**Bhagavats of the ten directions, the** the ubiquitous Buddhas who pervade the Universe

***bodhi*** see enlightenment

**Bodhidharma** in Zen mythology, the legendary Indian Buddhist master who brought Zen to China

**Bodhisattva** the Sanskrit for enlightened being. One who is on the Path to awakening; one who awakens others. The ideal to which Zen adherents aspire

**Buddha Nature** the True Nature which is the birthright of all beings and which all humans, enlightened or not, possess

**causation** the law of karma, of cause and effect, which deems that all deeds of body, speech and mind have future consequences for the perpetrator

**Ch'an** the original Chinese name for Zen

**Dao** see Tao

**deluded mind** the opposite of an enlightened mind

**Dharma** the teachings of the historical Buddha, Siddhartha Gautama, who is also known as Sakyamuni

***dhyana*** an Indian word meaning a profound inner stability and stillness of mind reached in meditation; closely related to *samadhi*

**enlightenment** the realization of one's true nature; the state attained after having become awakened to the Buddha's highest teaching; *bodhi* in Sanskrit

**Four Dhyana Heavens, the** the highest realms of unimaginable liberation, purity, harmony and wisdom; places of infinite height

**four obligations, the** to one's parents, to the sovereign, to people in general and to the three Buddhist treasures (the Buddha, the Dharma and the Sangha)

**Four Propositions, the** existing; not existing; both existing and not existing; neither existing nor not existing

***ge*-period** a practice period of 90 days, corresponding to the rainy season in India when monks were not allowed to travel

**Great Tripitaka, the** the collection of all the Buddhist writings including the *sutras*, precepts and commentaries

**Hantan** a second-century CE Chinese gentleman who lived in abject poverty, but never seemed worried by his plight

***ii*** exclamation indicating loud, contemptuous laughter

**Ino** the head chanter in a monastery

***kalpa*** a very long period of time, beyond human comprehension

**karma** see causation

***kensho*** the moment of enlightenment (in Rinzai Zen); seeing into one's essential nature and the nature of all things; also known as *satori*

**koan** a puzzle or "public case" used by Zen masters to help students to attain enlightenment

**Korei** a Chinese god who divided a mountain in two

**Kosei and Konan** two provinces in central China

**Kou** a courageous Chinese general

**Mahayana** one of three major Buddhist traditions, which is also called the Great Vehicle

**Maitreya** the future Buddha who will

come to save mankind 5,670 million years after Sakyamuni's death; often used to indicate the distant future

**Manjusri** the Bodhisattva of wisdom

**mindfulness** complete awareness in the present moment

***mondo*** questions and answers exchanged between Zen monks, expressing their Zen spirituality

**Mount Sumeru** the mountain in the centre of the universe, according to ancient Indian cosmology

**National Teacher, the** the title given to the emperor's Zen Master

***nii*** exclamation meaning "look!"

**Nirvana** a "blowing out," or extinction of the self; the state of enlightenment; sometimes refers to the supreme state of enlightenment attained by the Buddha

**One Hundred Negations, the** in Indian philosophy, the Four Propositions are multiplied until they eventually become One Hundred Negations

**Patriarchs, the** a long line of Zen Masters who were chosen to pass down the true teachings of Sakyamuni

**Pure Land, the** in True Pure Land Buddhism (a Japanese branch founded by Saint Shinrin), the world where believers are reborn

**rice-bag** a good-for-nothing or idler

**Rinzai Zen** a Japanese school of Zen that emphasizes the use of the koan

***sah*** sound made to indicate that one's voice has become hoarse

**Sakyamuni** the historical Buddha, founder of Buddhism, respected in Zen as the first human to attain enlightenment

**Sangha** the Buddhist priesthood

***satori*** see *kensho*

**Scented Ocean, the** an ocean of fragrant water on which, according to Buddhist cosmology, the world-system rests

**Shasanro** an illiterate fisherman who did not even know the alphabet

**shit-stick** phrase used to denote a disgusting or contemptible person or object

**shogun** a Japanese military dictator

**Soto Zen** a Japanese school of Zen that emphasizes the importance of *zazen*

***sutra*** a Buddhist text or discourse

**Tao** a Chinese word meaning the Path or Way, also known as Dao

***teisho*** a lecture by a master in the form of a commentary on one or more koans

***tenjin*** a snack, refreshments

***tenzo*** a high-ranking member of a monastery, in charge of the monks' meals

**three existences, the** in Indian tradition, the three realms of desire, form and no-form through which humans transmigrate in accordance with their karma

**turning word, the** a word of Truth; a word or phrase that has the power to turn delusion into enlightenment

**Vipasyin Buddha** the first of the seven Buddhas who preceded Sakyamuni; the Buddha of time immemorial

**Way, the** the Path to enlightenment, as described in Taoism and Buddhism

**World-Honored One, the** the Buddha, Sakyamuni, or Siddharta Gautama

**Yellow-faced Gotama** Sakyamuni

***zazen*** seated meditation

# CHRONOLOGY OF ZEN FIGURES

**Siddhartha Gautama** (c.563–483BCE) Indian, the historical Buddha (known as Sakyamuni Buddha after his enlightenment)

**Ananda** one of Sakyamuni's Ten Great Disciples and his attendant for 25 years

**Mahakasyapa** Indian disciple of the Buddha

**Bodhidharma** (d.532CE), 28th Dharma descendant of Siddhartha Gautama (Sakyamuni Buddha). Indian master who brought Zen to China, where he is known as the First Patriarch

**Hui-k'o** (Chinese monk, successor of Bodhidharma), the Second Patriarch to whom Bodhidharma passed down the teachings of Siddharta Gautama

**Hui-neng** (638–713) the Sixth Patriarch who became suddenly enlightened upon hearing the *Diamond Sutra*. All current Zen lineages are descended from him

**Shen-hui** (684–758) Chinese master

**Li Po** (701–762) Chinese poet

**Ch'iao-jan** (734–c.792) Chinese monk and poet

**Po Chu-i** (772–846) Chinese poet

**Han-shan** (active late 8th to early 9th century) Chinese poet

**T'ung-shan Liang-chieh** (807–869) Chinese master

**Wang An-shih** (1021–1086) Chinese statesman, scholar and poet

**Dangai** (dates unknown but c.1127–c.1279) Chinese poet

**Eisai** also called Yosai (1141–1215), introduced Zen into Japan

**T'ien-t'ung Ju-ching** (1163–1228) Chinese master

**Wu-men Hui-k'ai** known in Japanese as Mumon Ekai (1183–1260), Chinese master, compiled the *Gateless Gate* koan collection

**K'uo-an Shih-yuan** also referred to as Kakuan Shion (12th century), Chinese master of the Rinzai lineage

**Dogen** (1200–1253) founder of Japanese Soto Zen

**Ch'ing Kung** (d.1352) Chinese poet

**Shutaku** (1308–1388) Japanese master

**Ikkyu** (1394–1481) Japanese master and poet

**Reizan** (d.1411) Japanese poet

**Kodo** (1370–1433) Japanese poet

**Shubun** (active c.1423–1460) Japanese Zen monk of Shokoku-ji monastery in Kyoto

**Yin-yuan** (1592–1673) founder of the Obaku school

**Basho** (1644–1694) Japanese poet

**Kikaku** (1661–1707) Japanese poet, disciple of Basho

**Hakuin Ekaku** (1685–1769) revived and reformed Japanese Rinzai Zen

**Yayu** (1701–1783) Japanese poet

**Lady Chiyo-Jo** (1703–1775) Japanese poet

**Buson** (1715–1783) Japanese poet

**Kito** (1740–1789) Japanese poet

**Boryu** (18th century) Japanese poet

**Ryokan** (1757–1831) Japanese poet

**Soen Nakagawa** (1907–1984) Japanese poet

**Shinkichi Takahashi** (1901–1987) Japanese poet

**Sheng-yen** (b.1931) contemporary Chinese master

# FOR FURTHER READING


**Aitkin, R.** *Taking the Path of Zen.* San Francisco: North Point Press, 1982.

**Aitkin, R.**, transl. *The Gateless Barrier: The Wu-men Kuan (Mumonkan).* New York: North Point Press, 1991.

**App, U.** *Master Yunmen.* New York, Tokyo, London: Kodansha International, 1994.

**Blyth, R.H.** *Zen and the Zen Classics.* Tokyo: Hokuiseido Press, 1962.

**Cleary, T. and J.C.** *The Blue Cliff Record.* Boston: Shambhala, 1977.

**Cleary, T.** *Transmission of Light: Zen in the Art of Enlightenment.* San Francisco: North Point Press, 1990.

**Cleary, T.**, transl. *Unlocking the Zen Koan.* Berkeley: North Atlantic Books, 1997.

**Corless, R.J.** *The Vision of Buddhism: The Space Under the Tree.* New York: Pantheon, 1969.

**Foster, N. and Shoemaker**, eds. *The Roaring Stream: A New Zen Reader.* New Jersey: The Ecco Press, 1996.

**Harding, D.E.** *On Having No Head: Zen and the Re-discovery of the Obvious.* Harmondsworth: Arkana, 1986.

**Kapleau, P.** *The Three Pillars of Zen: Practice, Teaching and Enlightenment.* Boston: Beacon Press, 1965.

**Loori, J. D.** *Mountain Record of Zen Talks.* Boston: Shambhala, 1988.

**Low, A.** *An Invitation to Practice Zen.* Tokyo: Tuttle, 1989.

**Merzel, D.G.** *The Eye Never Sleeps: Striking to the Heart of Zen.* Massachusetts: Shambhala, 1991.

**Myoko-ni** *The Zen Way.* London: Zen Centre, 1987.

**Reps, P.**, ed. *Zen Flesh, Zen Bones.* Harmondsworth: Arkana, 1991.

**Ross, N.W.** *Buddhism: A Way of Life and Thought.* New York: Random House, 1980.

**Scott, D. and Doubleday, T.** *The Elements of Zen.* Dorset: Element Books, 1996.

**Seaton, J.P. and Malony, D.** *A Drifting Boat, Chinese Zen Poetry.* New York: White Pine Press, 1999.

**Sekida, K.** *Two Zen Classics: Mumonkan and Hekiganroku.* New York: Weatherhill, 1996.

**Sekida, K.** *Zen Training.* New York: Weatherhill, 1975.

**Sheng-yen**, transl. *The Poetry of Enlightenment: Poems by Ancient Ch'an Masters.* New York: Dharma Drum Publications, 1987.

**Shibayama, Z.** *Zen Comments on the Mumonkan.* New York: Mentor, 1974.

**Stryk, L. and Ikemoto, T.**, eds. *The Penguin Book of Zen Poetry.* London: Penguin Books, 1981.

**Suzuki, D.T.** *Manual of Zen Buddhism.* New York: Grove Press, 1978.

**Suzuki, D.T.** *Zen and Japanese Culture.* Princeton: Princeton University Press, 1970.

**Suzuki, S.** *Zen Mind Beginners' Mind.* New York: Weatherhill, 1970.

**Tanahshi, K. and Schneider, D.**, eds. *Essential Zen.* New York: Harper Collins, 1994.

**Tanahshi, K.**, ed. *Moon in a Dewdrop: Writings of Zen Master Dogen.* San Francisco: San Francisco Zen Center, 1985.

**Watson, B.** *Ryokan: Zen Monk-Poet of Japan.* New York: Columbia University Press, 1977.

**Yamada, K.** *Gateless Gate.* Tuscon: University of Arizona Press, 1979.

# TEXT ACKNOWLEDGMENTS

The Publishers wish to thank Calen Rayne for his help in selecting the poems and the following for their kind permission to reproduce the translations and other copyright material in this book. Every effort has been made to trace copyright owners, but if anyone has been omitted we apologize and will, if informed, make corrections in any future printings.

**Poems**

pp.23, 26, 28, 29 and 37 from *A Drifting Boat, Chinese Zen Poetry* by Jerome P. Seaton and Dennis Maloney (Freedinia, NY, White Pine Press, 1999), reproduced by permission of White Pine Press; p.24 from *The T'ang Poet-monk, Chiao-jan* by Thomas P. Nielson (Tempe, Arizona 85281: Center for Asian Studies, Arizona State University, 1972), reproduced by permission of the Center for Asian Studies, Arizona State University; pp.30, 33 (top and bottom), 38, 43, 44, 46 (top and bottom), 47 (top), 48 (left and right), 51, 52 (left and right), 53 (left and right), 54 (left, middle and right) and 66 from *The Penguin Book of Zen Poetry* edited and translated by Lucien Stryk and Takashi Ikemoto (Penguin Books, 1981), reproduced by permission of Lucien Stryk; pp.34, 47 (bottom), 60, 63, 65 and 69 from *Essential Zen* edited by Kazuaki Tanahashi and David Schneider, copyright © 1994 by Kazuaki Tanahashi and David Schneider, illustrations copyright © 1994 by Kazuaki Tanahashi, reprinted by permission of HarperCollins Publishers, Inc.; pp.40 and 41 from *Wild Ways: Zen Poems of Ikkyu* translated by John Stevens, © 1995, reprinted by arrangement with Shambhala Publications, Inc., Boston; pp.56–9 from *Penetrating Laughter* by Kazuaki Tanahashi, copyright © 1982 by Kazuaki Tanahashi, published by The Overlook Press, 2568 Rte. 212, Woodstock, NY 12498, (914) 679-6838.

***The Gateless Gate***

pp.72–143 from *Zen Comments on the Mumonkan* by Zenkei Shibayama, English language translation copyright © 1974 by Zenkei Shibayama, reprinted by permission of HarperCollins Publishers, Inc.

**The *Ox-Herding Pictures***

pp.146–55 from *Essential Zen* as above.

# PHOTOGRAPHIC ACKNOWLEDGMENTS

The Publishers would like to thank the following people, photographic libraries and museums for permission to reproduce their material. Every care has been taken to trace copyright holders. However, if we have omitted anyone we apologize, and will, if informed, make corrections in any future printings.

**2** Images; **9** Magnum / Rene Burri; **14** Corbis / Paul A. Berry; **22** Getty/Stone Images; **25** Photonica / Yukari Ochiai; **27** Florentine Schwabbauer, Germany; **28–9** Getty/Stone Images; **31** Getty/Stone Images; **32** Photonica / Shouichi Itoga; **35** Getty/Stone Images; **38–9** Images; **42** Photonica / Shouichi Itoga; **44–5** Photonica / Takeshi Odawara; **49** Photonica / Masao Ota; **50** Tessa Traeger; **52–3** Images; **55** Natural History Photograhic Agency; **61** Images; **62** Photonica / Shinichi Eguchi; **64** Photonica / Shooting Star; **67** Images; **68** Tessa Traeger; **72–3** Tessa Traeger; **76** Photonica / Jun Kishimoto; **80** Hulton Getty; **82–3** Photonica / Katsumi Suzuki; **84–5** Tessa Traeger; **89** Photonica / H. Okamoto; **90–1** Images; **94** Photonica / Alan Sirulnikoff; **99** Photonica / Nara; **102–3** Photonica / Yuko Shimada; **104–5** Photonica / Shouichi Itoga; **109** Photonica / Patrick Clark; **110** Photonica / Shouichi Itoga; **114–5** Images; **119** Tessa Traeger; **122** Photonica / Alex Maclean; **127** Getty/Stone Images; **129** Getty/Stone Images; **130–1** Photonica / Elaine Mayes; **138** Getty/Stone Images; **140–1** Photonica / Michael Gesinger; **143** Images; **146–55** Shokuku-ji Temple, Kyoto, Japan. Photo courtesy of the Kyoto National Museum, Japan.